ECHOES OF LOVE

PROF.K.RAMAKRISHNA

Contents

Contents

Contents

Foreword

Welcome to loving hearts Everlasting in creation is love.

This beautiful concept is seen from ancient Puranas, Epics, Poems to modern poetry.

In other words, it is making all branches of literature its own. It is universally true that there are those who do not enjoy this universal feeling of love.

Love has the power to lift even those who are pushed into the abyss as high as the Himalayas.

Loving is an art! Lucky to be loved.

In Telugu poetry, love appears in essays beyond the dose, but in emotional poetry, it leaves an indelible mark on the hearts of lovers and rises to a noble level in the hands of poets like Raiprolu. Such an incredible feeling is "LOVE",

So... all that I put on paper as this poems,which I swayed in my imagination... I put it in one place and give it to you.

Enjoy them Heartfully

- Prof.K.Ramakrishna.

Preface

<u>ECHOES OF YOUNG HEARTS</u>

As John Keats said, "If poetry comes not as naturally as the leaves to a tree, it had better not come at all." In essence, poetry should emerge effortlessly from the poet's soul, much like how a tree naturally produces leaves. If it requires excessive force, it is not true poetry. True poetry endures through the ages. John Milton, Wordsworth, Keats, Shelley, and Byron created timeless works of poetry. From Indian English literature, Tagore's Gitanjali is equally eternal.

Prof. Ramakrishna's pen has sprouted the boughs of love, blossoming into poetic flowers.

His poetry collection, Prema Naa Chirunama, truly aligns with the essence defined above. Though categorized as fiction, every poem in the collection is a reflection of youthful experiences. Notably, poetic citations like Ontari Thanapu Chikatilo, Ekkada Unnavu?, Nenu?!, and others stand as fine examples of his poetic prowess. The lines, "The body may disappear, but love remains as a shining star in the darkness. (Surviving through your memories)" haunt you every time you read them. We can't stop in the middle once we start reading this book. If it had not been translated into English, the global audience would have definitely missed these poems.

A translator must carry forward the essence and depth of the original poetry. Here, translator Ms. Preethi Richards has done her job exceptionally well. The title "Echoes of Love" itself showcases her mastery of translation. In one instance, she translated the word Chirunama as Lable!—how apt! Even idioms and complex poetic expressions have been beautifully rendered by Preethi.

I congratulate both the original poet, Prof. Ramakrishna, and the translator, Ms. Preethi Richards, for their commendable contributions to the field of poetry. I hope more literature is translated from Telugu to English, allowing local culture and heritage to reach a global audience.

With best wishes,

Prof.U.Umesh Kumar

Vice Chancellor

1. Love is my label

For Life Love is the label,
For Love Sacrifice is the label,
The mind addresses Both love and sacrifice,
For Mind Affection is the label,
A life without love is A Letter without address.

2. In the dark of loneliness

Am alone in this darkness of loneliness
Whenever the heart is cut by a saw in the darkness of
loneliness...
Like the pain of a stone hitting the little finger.....
like a baby who won't leave the mother's lap......
For you, The eyes and mouths open vertically...
Seeking for your love...
Your soft hands yearn for the touch of your fingers.
One day's worth of your pure love is enough for My life!
I close my eyes comfortably and will enter into the Paradise..!

3. Beloved take this letter

Beloved! ... Take this letter!

Beloved...! Take this letter! The line of my heart's deepest thoughts! Your form has become the dream that adorns my mind. Your memories run like letters, racing through my soul. Your words stalk my path, tormenting me. Your love alone has shaped itself into my poetry.

When you appear, this suffering finds relief; when you show mercy, this sorrow finds rest.

Every dawn, I wait eagerly for your arrival... patiently... my heart's flower withered. The fragrance of hope has vanished. In the dawn without you, 'dawn' itself flew away. My mind shattered, leaving only fragments. Like a desert, I stand alone... solitary!

Your words are my reward, your song my honor; without them, only the cry of rejection, a tale of despair, would tear my life apart.

Did the sweetness of past affection turn into bitter grief? Have sharp words become arrows in this contest? Will silence ever break? Can the one who was once lost ever be made whole again?

4. Sweet memories

The sweet moments we spent together
Were the sour wounds that burn the forest of the heart,
The potion we drank together Today, became my sweet poison
All the steps I walked with you... Were written and faded in the
annals of history
Every letter that's been scribbled started mocking at me,
That I have been struck..!
What can I say my friend!
Those sweet memories of those days
Were like never used fragrant jasmines
You became a voice and Uttered praises through me, And I am
with your help,
Had became a consonant and mumbled with flowers.
Until the creation of unity sentences, Our phrases will remain as
sweet memories.

5. In the darkness of loneliness

Am alone in this darkness of loneliness
Whenever the heart is cut by a saw in the darkness of
loneliness...
Like the pain of a stone hitting the little finger.....
like a baby who won't leave the mother's lap......
For you The eyes and mouths open vertically...
Seeking for your love...
Your soft hands yearn for the touch of your fingers.
One day's worth of your pure love is enough for My life!
I close my eyes comfortably And will enter into the Paradise..!

6. The world is full of love

If you wish hard to love on necessity then it is not love
Love is not commercial! Love is the natural resource of arid
life…..
Love is like a rebirth…
Love… Is like a climber that woven tightly to the tree
, The whole world is through Love, I love this love, and for this
love.
In the inhales and exhales there is love,
There is love in the beats if the heart, Mother loves her child,
Likewise a child loves this universe. Love…. There is no expiry
date for you Love,
There is not even a manufactory date,
You are an infinite abstract feeling, Which is experienced
through seniority
. Even if the time moves , Even if the body twists and turns, The
symbols of this love Remains eternal.
A Tajmahal, A hyderabad city, A Qutubminar,
Everything is a symbol of Love The world is love.
Love… You are a monist, An Infinite peace,
Whether it may be, Radha-Madhav, Paru-Devadas,
Laila-Majnu, Romeo - juliet,
Whoever else it may be, Before love the whole universe is a speck.

Love, It has no desire to appetite.. Nor sleep,
It doesn't have any time bound... nor money Love is a feeling
beyond words can reach,
It resides in the deep layers of heart, It's a jewel studded in the
heart,
In fact the whole world is filled with love,
If not love, then this whole world would be in confusion.

7. Beloved...! Why is this love

Beloved...!

Why do I love you so? When you reside in my heart, an indescribable joy fills me, an endless delight.

My heart hums with silent melodies, a thousand unspoken songs. Every whisper seems to be a call meant only for me. Every breeze feels like it is singing softly to my soul.

How can I offer the blooming flowers of love, the harvest of affection from within me, to your feet?

It is the glory of humanity that awakened my soul! It is you who shaped me into 'who I am'!

In the emptiness that once consumed me, you sang songs of enthusiasm, filling me with vibrant energy.

Beloved!

You are an extraordinary force, a tonic that gives a thousand-fold strength, a melody that touches the very core of hearts. You are the lightning that stirs the dormant minds from slumber!

Beloved!

In my quest to understand you, I became a tiny droplet in the endless river of love. To converse silently, mysteriously, across the

expanse of two souls—that is love.
Beloved!
Every time I speak to you, it feels like waves rise and crash,
speaking softly to the grains of sand in secret.
You stand by me, like a mountain, offering unwavering support,
and in your presence, I find my victory.
Beloved!
The fragrance of the air loves the wind.
The river loves the ocean.
The night loves the moon.
And I... that is why I love you!

8. Good bye dear

Beloved!... seeking refuge in you,
I have come to remember you, is it the faultless love?
Those flowers and the nectars
The forests and the dusky tunes are lost today,
Your love net has descended in the layer of the my mind,
You made my agony as yours, And my happiness as yours,
And you light the lamp of your love in my heart, with your smile
Now if I ask why are you laughing? Even if you want to laugh,
our love experience bonds Your pale bonds hold you back and
disturb me
I am surrounded by dry trees,burned remnants, pain, broken
heart, living in love, acting in life,
How will you laugh if I ask you now? Laughter is our bond of
love
Your soft bonds hold you back and disturb you for me.
I was surrounded by dead trees, burnt corpses, anguish, and a
broken heart.
Even if you act in life, learn to live in love!
The solution to this life and death problem is you ... your love!
It's up to you!

9. Tree of love

The seeds of Vision Will arise and Germinate in the field Of heart
They see the Roots Of feelings,
The names of the feelings are The joys of the love,
Words becomes the branches,
Songs becomes the shoots,
Looking forward, With the eyes open,
And finally the fruit Of Love matures
And falls into the Lap.

10. For You

For you,
Every moment of this life is for you, every moment,
Moment by moment, my longing is always for you.
The sweetness of my love, like a buzzing bee,
Spins around you in every direction, lost in your attraction.
Ready for any test, I am!
For the memory of your love, like the full moon's glow.
For you, my breath; for you, my thoughts,
Oh crescent moon-like beauty! Why is it that...
I rush forward, offering all my love to you!

11. Silent Blossom

Silent Blossom

In the forest of love, a flower bloomed, braving the scorching
summer heat.
The silent bloom of the flower, under the full moon's glow,
The hum of the bee, an offering to love,
The buzzing of sweet nectar, a barrier to the winds of the night.
Oh, the beauty nature spreads!
You've bound my eyes and feet,
Leaving only the paths of tears to wander.
Silence is the flower's gaze,
Do you know, my heart, that silence is the union of souls?
Knowing this, why this weariness upon me,
Oh, beauty! Why this soft whisper?
The silent song of the heart breathes life into the soul.

12. The identity of Love

Love has no caste and no religion,
Like Blood that flows in all languages and in all religions
Like Breathing, Which is natural in life, Love is same.
To the slaying wind,
To the rising sun, to the soothing moon,
To the black cloud that rains, .
What is their caste?
What is their religion? caste- religion Language-dressing
Whatever it may be, Moving together in the ocean of love,
With full of sincerity And full of embodied knowledge,
Love floats within us.

13. The Agony of my heart

*The innocent, the immortal lover is like a magnet Fascinated
and glittered,*

I was deceived before I knew that everything was a li

e I invited you with an open heart I worshiped his face with joy

*There were no tears left in the wet eyes after the filth was
splashed*

*Broken strings and broken harps are making the noise of
memories*

In the broken mirror of dedicated life

Sweets sneer in smoldering venom Mirror pieces are proud

He made assumptions Close to love

Burned life Affection is the only cure for this mental illness.

14. One stone is enough!...

Life is a journey which is Survived by the tide of experience.
My passing life shed water where there was no water and left
tears.
It was like a fish thrown on the shore, And the heart which
should comfort me,
Confronted me instead! I am not an amphibious creature like
you.
You could stay anywhere You wish to,
You have robbed me of everything and blocked me,
One stone is enough for Life is a great challenge,
how many waves of turmoil have poured out,
how many precious moments have been watered to touch the
heart.
One match is enough To set a fire to the forest
Like a stone in the hands of a madman
I gave my heart to your hand. You made me crazy,
Even you want to be green... You have twisted the net,
you have lost faith in victory my friend.

15. Dear friend

Friend! The sweet essence of your humorous words has digested into my soul more deliciously than honey.

The portrait of your face is etched in me, surpassing the glory of spring. Do you know why you remain in my thoughts? Because everything I see reflects you.

Your radiant dawn has sown fresh dreams in my heart. Like the rays of the sun, your lively spirit has injected my heart with "D" vitamins.

Every time you vowed to make me cry, I ended up laughing, for I lost the game. Do you remember the wager we made?

If I win, I'll love you! If you win, you must love me!

Like the stars in the sky, blooming wild flowers in the forest, the golden moonlight shining through the mist,

You stand tall in my heart's mountains, conquering me with the flowers of your smile.

The pain of your memories swirls around like a gentle breeze, echoing in my silent tears, nurturing the ink of my quiet grief.

16. Don't hold the Breath

Is the heart broken!

Does the affection lost

! Until the very moment of yesterday,

There was a soul, who claimed to be there for you,

Did it loose the sight of you? Don't let go the hope,

Don't hang on to your breath, Be patient for your comfort.

Look at the thousands of people ,

Who are waiting at your heart's corner,

Welcome them to break the limits of your selfishness

Somewhere a heart comes, looking for you to breath new life..!

17. Where have you been?

In the doorway of your eyes, I am the rainbow;
In the beats of your heart, I am the silent sound.
I am the shine of my beauty, and you are the light.
You are the heroine of my sweet dreams,
The queen of my thoughts, the gentle one,
Your glances, your shy smiles,
Your lips, your eyes, your melodious voice,
A beautiful, strange companion,
You are the vision in my heart's eyes.
You came softly, gently,
You nurtured and captured endless love,
I've fallen.
I forgot the sky and the earth.
You filled my being entirely,
You touched my back,
Held me like a tree,
Pulled me through thorny paths,
And showed me a way through the hardest roads.
Where have you been?
Where have you been?
Wherever you are, just being with you is enough for me, a
thousand times more.

18. Illusion

Illusion, illusion!! Everything is illusion,
You, in your cruelty, wounded me,
You placed all the unbearable burdens on my heart,
Is there a heaven in the palm of your hand?
With your enchanting gaze, you evaporated my soul.
My heart, a temple, burned with the fire of sacrifice,
While you turned me into ashes.
I sought you, like a beggar,
And when the winds of the earth blow,
Or the rivers flow,
Your melody is an unmatched fragrance
That fills the air with its sweet scent.
Why did you step forward,
When I had already lost everyone to you?
Do you have ears but cannot hear?
Do you have eyes but cannot see?
Will you leave me behind?
Can you reject me, the story you've created?
Knowing that I was an innocent fool,
Why did you decide to bind me with chains,
And cast away all the love in the well of your indifference?

19. Acceptance

A heart like the moon,
You came to me, calling me,
Though I looked beyond, though I gave so much,
I built a temple for you in my heart,
And placed my life's light before you.
You, a jewel shining brightly,
Have you turned into a stone?
You, once as sweet as sugar,
Have you now become a thorn?
Have you entangled the beautiful heart
In the nets of a stranger's web?
Like a storm, does your mind create chaos?
Are all the memories lost in your madness?
Only when death strikes,
And destiny shifts,
Will you change your tune?
Will you accept it with love?

20. The Pupil of the Eye

The pen touched the paper,
The thought gave birth to words,
Melodies bloomed as songs,
And love wove poetry into the air.
Our timeless friendship,
Its fragrance of love,
Became a sweet perfume.
Through the glance of the eyes,
I gathered the harvest of affection,
Each gaze, a spark of joy!
Playful words are the fertilizer for this crop,
Love is the water for this bloom,
A smile, the first dew drop,
A joyful radiance,
And the moon that has given me its light.
Is this all? Is there more?
No, I cannot sleep,
For my eyes cannot rest!
The age of childish innocence,
Longing for companionship,
Is rushing toward union.
As I looked at you,

Did my eye become the pupil,
Captivated by you?
Did you win my heart?

• 23 •

21. Thoughts

It is your thoughts that wakes up
Sleep melts with your thought
Your imagination stopped the hunger
Thirst quenched with your call.
My Love for you starts like a small candle light Expands and
grows into a big fire,
If I stand before you assuming as a droplet of rain,
It combines and forms into a thunderstorm.
As Minutes melts like water drops..
I am becoming a man of indecisiveness
Do I have to get wet this year? Do you have to burn in the fire?
With your short glance, I can forget All these rains are fires I can
forget myself!

22. I See Myself in You.

The scorching heat of my age,
Finds solace in the "oasis" of your gaze,
Your smile, the dawn of comfort,
Has granted me a brief respite.
"Ahh!" Today, I could finally breathe easy!
The winds of struggle and turmoil have softened,
And my heart, in its slow rhythm,
Plays the beat of calm,
With every soft thump.
Around the tender branches of your love,
My eyelashes flutter,
As memories, like gentle waves,
Touch me and soothe my soul.
Do you know why all of this is happening?
Because, now, you—
Are not just you,
But I see myself in you!

23. Sweet song

You are a sweet song,
Made up of verses of heart,
And the stanzas of love,
You are a song of fullmoon shine,
Having your own lipi and music!
You move and leave me I can't be with you,
I'm full of search I am the voice and you are the tantri
and you are the veena and I am the flower
and you are the flower The song sung is ours
The song of life is ours Our old song of tears should not be in the
game of fate

24. Surviving by your memories..

The body may disappear, but love remains as a shining star in the darkness,
The first step may always be the small one,
but for thousands of steps it will be the guide,
each step is the beginning of a journey of thousands of miles.
A breath may be short, but it sustains life Each drop together becomes the great river,
Even if the two letters or those two syllables that come from the heart are full of words,
And those two words are enough to sing songs of awakening,
Those two words of yours knock The chambers of my heart,
These flowing memories will save Me from the death.

25. I am In you

Whenever I talk to you How pure How natural it felt...
Like, the backyard of this house,
the lips are like a bunch of sprouted plants,
Whenever your cold words Reaches this sensitive heart
My heart is injured it gets cold chills.
As flowers smile... In a chorus of sounds and this Foggy thoughts
it takes me into a trance....
Everyday you try to leave me..
You are getting closer.
From the moment you said a temporary goodbye.
You in me and you in me!!
We are overwhelmed with abstract feelings!!!

26. I see myself in you

he scorching heat of my age,
Finds solace in the "oasis" of your gaze,
Your smile, the dawn of comfort,
Has granted me a brief respite.
"Ahh!" Today, I could finally breathe easy!
The winds of struggle and turmoil have softened,
And my heart, in its slow rhythm,
Plays the beat of calm,
With every soft thump.
Around the tender branches of your love,
My eyelashes flutter,
As memories, like gentle waves,
Touch me and soothe my soul.
Do you know why all of this is happening?
Because, now, you—
Are not just you,
But I see myself in you!

27. To combine Body and soul

What has been with you for so many ages
and you don't know this moment,
are you forgetting the moments
or the years we spent together?
The moment that proved
that those sweet moments are unforgettable...rare...
the moment that has been blessed for me
for a hundred years again,
is my mind moved? Or Is it time?
No, what is frozen is my breathe!
Endless blessings to you...
Is it possible for us to stop it?
It is in our power to stop?
This is the word of both minds.
The cutting of the burning bosom......
The boiling moments ignited
The unquenchable desire ,
The penitent virginity.
While you are losing your grip
and crying that you can't do it anymore,

I told to bind it with time.
When this fight started
I didn't even let my dreams come close,
Fearing where this body denies this soul!
There are still a few moments left for both of us to wait for ,
When this body and soul and United through marriage!

28. You Are Myself

Whenever my heart's desire demanded,
The price of your lips rose higher.
And as the price rose,
The supply of my words diminished.
In my heart, there was an unmanageable stockpile,
In the black market of dreams, I stole my own emotions.
There are no alternatives, no substitutes,
For the object of my desire. You, and only you!
No competitive markets exist for us—
None can rival us.
Do not be indifferent; my entire effort
Is devoted to earning your goodwill!
Here, there is no room for diminishing returns!
No exceptions, no compromises—
No obstacles can stand in the way of love!
It's all a singular truth!
Everything that exists is "You alone!"

29. Dear Love

Why do you hide your face?
Do you want to Get away from me?
Remembering you all the time in my heart...
Am waiting for you If I have wings on my chest, I used to fly and
stand before of you,
Your image, your smile, The juggling of your words
They made me yours without letting me knew,
Your great silence... Made my heart like raging storms in the
ocean,
A heart whose size is of my little fist Did I deny anything that
you asked?
Any nerve...or not?
If you have asked I would Decorate your palms!
With The blue clouds that are in the sky
The blood that runs in my nerves will be fixed on your face like
Tilak!
I will decorate your hair with the flowers, That are plucked from
the sky of stars!
It will stop any time it is running! And I will bind that time in
your tight fist!!!
I am yours until my last breath... Still you are silent? in that
silence I explore- millions of tunes,

You just "Keep looking "
When you- are in me And - when I am in you,
We are the same What should I say to you?
"If you open the door of your heart, You will see me remembering
you"!

30. Search

Search My eyes,
turning the page of sensations and memories
searching for years for you,
A pair of other souls greeted this non-stop eye travel...
This might be the end for travel of my eyes The final stage...!

31. Dear

Do you hear my silent songs in your ears??
Are the memories of my love moving in your mind??
Do you see my sweet marks on your legs??
Your eyes make me restless!
Your pranks are adding to my worries
You are all my future sky and shower the Sparks of full moon!

32. Musings

You never said a word,
Neither I did,
But it was the Silence,
Who spoke the unuttered words.
It shared the musings of our love,
You never said anything about your feelings,
But I understood each and Everything of them,
Because it was your eyes That communicated with my heart.
I found a life in that eyes,
I found a hope in that eye To love you more and more.

33. There are no words infront of you

When you stand before me,
I wanted to talk a lot.
But I Couldn't speak when you stood in front of me!!
It's not that the words don't come,
but the sweetness of the words should be hidden tightl

34. I am always amazed

Are you unintelligible and uninterrogative!
You look like an unblossomed bud,
After a while you will be like a dried up model.
And all the dynamism will be yours
You turn me into a lifeless rock and make me a palace
What an unintelligible question you are! I am always surprised!

35. Love Has No Selfishness

Do not lay your tricks upon me,
Do not cast your gaze like weapons upon me...
In the depth of that desire,
Your warm embrace, your smiling flowers
Bloom in the garden of my heart...
A song echoed softly,
Desire, like a waterfall,
Your love, like a snowstorm,
Your memories ring through the silence,
And I feel lost, in agony!
Do you see me now, in pity?
Why, why, did you meet me?
Your form has made me still,
Around you, my thoughts weave endlessly.
New hopes bloom like flowers,
Their wings fluttering, spinning in playful chaos.
After reading your letter, my eyes became like rivers,
They rained in silence... why?
Why do you love me so deeply?
What have I given you?

Yet, even in my madness,
Can love ever have selfishness?

• 41 •

36. Love is versatile

Beloved!
If you get angry
, you will look dull and Your state moves my heart,
If you are calm,
you will look tender and hug me.
In whatever form you may be in
And Whatever juice you may drink
In whatever character are you living in?
Love in your eyes... is reflected in many ways.

37. Barrier

Barrier With waves of reluctance,
in the bosom of hardships
With a rising uppeal Suffocating During breathlessness
I Found a kind collaboration
A warm touch of warmth
Since then it is a new feeling,
In the slaying wind, In singing swallows
In the blooming lotus
In the raining cloud
In the shining stars
You are everywhere
Among the paraceliacs
You are all the moon!
Why is there a barrier between you and me?
Is there is screen between Water lilly and Moon,
Lotus and sun,
Cloud and the drops?
Is there a screen?
Tell me,
dear open your mind,
Look into yourself,
Don't you have me?

This man's heart is dedicated To this women,
Don't do this to me women,
Don't play me with time,
Removing this barrier is a difficult task!

38. Warmth of tears

Dear you,

What should I write?

What I am supposed to write?

You are in me

And I am in you,

In the deepest layers of heart,

We are unite..!

The little to be written,

and the little to be said!

Words aren't enough

For this affectionate dearness,

You sit in front of me And tease me,.

Why do you throw your love mesh upon me?

I never knew the greatness Of the single touch,

sight.... And the words,

I learnt this from you,

I can't stand either of this happiness,

Or sadness, But this happy tears rolled out of me..

The greatness of the warmth lies in this tears.

39. Friend! Love!

I will be around you like,
A Breathe in your breath,
A step in your path Eyeball in your eyes,
A feel in your words,
Sweet dreams in your sleep,
Tears in your agony,
And you You wrapped and touched me.
Like a five-moon parrot
before my eyes every night,
Like a butterfly of green light,
like a blue flower,
like a clove,
like a white milk quail,
you touch me,
You sing to me even in my sleep.
You light up your mane like a harp,
what a genius!
Can't you have compassion for a little while,
after giving breath to these imaginations?
Sincerely, my mind is deceived,
unstoppable heart-drops evaporated
and shed tears. but,

whatever, it may be
Don't you come? Either as Friend Or as love!!!

40. Broken solitude

Like Vishvamitra
when he was lonely
Silent penance is freed by the blessings of your words,
All the silent rocks froze
and melted like ice
In the heart of the establishment
with a collaborative approach,
The glory of morning tunes were heard,
The dead face tree is full of laughter whispering
All these years of silence,
just for this moment?
In the cage of the eyes
where all the feelings are intertwined,
I have imprisoned all the structures made by time.
Before the heart lamp was dry,
before the young saffron was used
the miserable moments of waiting,
before the last moment was pronounced,
Beloved Welcome to you !
With the showers of love!

41. I can forget myself

42. Tears hidden behind the eyes

That there are so many tears behind these eyes
Which I am unaware of ituntill I waited for you
That this mind hides so many sorrows in itself.
You don't know until you search your mind,
If I knew that you were hurt
Then I would become a living sculpture!
The thought that revolves around you
is windy Reluctantly locked behind the eyelids
You are the same in dreams even if I don't sleep!
Even if I wake up from dreams,
that will be along with your memories
They appear every moment.
Mocking my lonely self these days.
A scene silently slipping before the eyes...
Spilling from the eye sockets
Before each drop combines and forms into an ocean
And before it overwhelms me
I wish to see you I wish to say you something,
That the Teardrops hidden behind the eyes
Communicating secretly!

43. Desire, is like a Waterfall

Desire, is like a waterfall,
A song so sweet, yet unsung...
A playful, tender bond,
Like a honeyed connection,
An unbroken fragrance of love.
The moonlight's soft gaze
Blends with the earth in unity.
The eyes that greet,
The lips that speak,
The body that trembles,
The love that sparkles—
Hidden beneath the storm,
Whispers that speak of tomorrow,

44. To Unite US

For so many ages, it has been your garden,
Yet, does this moment still elude you?
Are these fleeting moments passing like seconds,
Or are they the years we've spent together?
Those sweet, cherished moments—
Impossible to forget,
Rare, they have proven their worth—
A moment that has granted me a hundred years of blessings,
Did my heart stir? Was it time?
No, it was the breath that ceased and then moved
With boundless longing, for you.
Is this our time to stop?
It stopped on its own,
This is the voice of two hearts.
The longing of hearts...
The burning moments have ignited
An unquenchable thirst,
The purity of youthful innocence is slipping away.
As helplessness takes over,
I can't escape it,
While the struggle continues.
As dreams can't even reach the proximity of the fight,

Where are you, where is your heart,
Is it drawing us apart?
These moments we still wait for,
They are meant for the sweet days ahead,
When 'You' and 'I will break their boundaries.
The fight that began in the heart
Won't let dreams come closer.
Where are you, where is your heart,
Is it drawing us apart?
These moments we still wait for,
They are meant for the sweet days ahead,
When 'You' and 'I' will break their boundaries.

45. Love and Me

If Love is a wonderful work of art,
Then I am Ravi Varma.
If Love is a sweet poem,
Then I am Kalidasa.
If Love is a musician
Then I am AR Rahman
. If Love is a magic,
Then I am PC Sarkar.
If Love is a dance,
Then I am Lawrence.
If Love is blind
Then I am Louis Braille.
If Love is a gift of compassion,
Then am Theresa.
If Love is a game,
Then am a winning horse.
If Love is a white paper,
Then I am a sweet pen.
This Love is such an ocean of consciousness
then I am a single droplet in it.

46. An Empty world

Oh dear!
As the rays of twilight draw near,
And the roaring of mid-day sounds,
And the whirlwinds blow the rain,
and the ocean waves roll in.
This heart is bursting,
And i will not forget it,
As the love God shots the arrows
, The rain God pours rain,
Your moon- shaped face appears
and hopes bloom for unattainable beauty.
This heart is beating and this word is turning away
As sweet jingles are heard, sweet voices are threatened,
and your beautiful heart disappears.
This heart beats on this side.

47. First drop of rain..

Your love dripped on the desolate heartland
and the whole earth trembled once.
Your passion has stirred storms
in the hollows of my heart.
In your memories,
The snow and ice melted on top of the rock heart,
No matter how much she screams,
she can raise her voice
when she is anxious.
No wind, no touch, no smile, no flower,
wherever I look, there you are....
Your love is taking me away, I am alone in my desert,
And I am quenching my thirst
with you With New inspiration.

48. Natural

How natural is love!
Whenever you touch me...
It's like touching mother earth on a rainy evening.
Every time you shake me....
It is like a child of the mother
of the river leaping to take the wave to the shore and play
. Whenever you see me...
it's like a full moon surrounded by lilies of the valley.....
whenever you walk with me...
like two hearts playing silent lyre strings....
whenever you dream of me...
All the roots of the soil come up
Flowers and pods It is as if the head is covered with small twigs.
How natural! How natural!!
How natural is love?
Pure like mother's milk!!
And pure like a Laughter of a baby!

49. Around the lotus

Around the lotus, the mud clings,
Poison surrounds the shore of the shrub,
A short-lived bride spins around,
Thorns pierce the soft petals of the rose,
Water flows through the thorns of the bushes,
Even stones are hurt by them!
The deity created this,
A lock that refuses to open,
A voice that cannot be heard.
All the rare beauties come as gifts,
Yet they bind you without giving their true essence.
A heart's pain that words cannot express—
No language can capture its depth!
Who can extinguish the fire in the heart with sweet words?
Who dares to challenge fate's verdict?

50. Thank you

Thank you Dear Friend!
The chemicals of your funny words
are digested in me sweeter than honey.
Your voice is colorful which is Imprinted in me like the head of
spring.
Do you know why I remember you?
Because you are all that I could see
You are my favorite morning
A new chapter has opened up in my mind.
Your movement like sunshine injected vitamin "D" into his
heart.
Whenever you tried to make me cry,
I wanted you to laugh,
Remember the bet for the game we used to play?
If I win I will love you!
If you win you have to love me!!
You stood in the hills of my heart,
You won me over with the flowers of your smile.
The pain of your memories is swirling
around like a river, while my silence is making me cry.

51. The moment I saw you,

Ask the time,
about the moment
I saw you,
Ask this heartbeat
about the time
it skipped a beat for you,
Look at your priceless form
that is marked upon my heart,
Ask my thoughts
about the love that created for you,
You are a strong addiction to my heart
dear Love, No matter whom you ask,
No matter what you ask,
This heart beats for you,
Untill the last moment it could!

52. How do i love you?

53. Am struck

I was struck by the sudden moment,
The sudden moments of beauty
Wandering around me,
When she moved around me
The wind slayed her beauty,
The flowers in the garden whispered,
To their neighbours about her beauty,
The heart strings played a music of love chords,
The chirping of birds sang a note of love for this man,
She seemed to hear that song,
So she stood by my side and laughed at me!
Oh! This beauty! I am struck by her smile!

54. Gift

Climbed from road,
Thinking of what gift I could give you,
I Found myself on the land,
Land filled with flowers,
The wild flowers are everywhere
Hosting the honey bees and flies,
Butterflies dancing among them,
These flowers remind me of you,
Dear girl, these would serve you
As a precious gift,
I know you would dance
To this music of bees,
To the slaying of winds,
I know nothing can be as worthy
as This beauty, As worthy as this present.

55. Red Rose

A Red Rose
In the fearful garden,
Lay in the middle
Filled with green grass,
A red rose plant
Stood there fearlessly,
Growing inch by inch
Day by day, Spreading the beauty,
It stood there
In the hardest days,
In the hardest times,
In the meanest hours
Without losing hope,
This Red rose,
Was a gifted plant By you,
Reminding me of you,
Am writing this letter By the virtue of this rose.

56. Poems

These poems are the Things I do,
In the dark nights,
These poems are the Words of my love,
Arranged like Beads of the pearls,
These poems are the Messengers
between You and my love,
These words are the Light that reaches your heart,
These words are like
The stones glimmering in The lakes and ponds
In between the running water,
I am like a saint who looks for God everywhere,
I look for you in between these words of poems.

57. Today

Today again my heart made a wish,
Today again I explained it,
Not to hold this hope,
Today again it denied it.
Today again my heart made wish,
Today again I explained it,
Not to love you more and more,
Today again it denied it.
Today again my heart made a wish,
Today again I explained it,
Not to wish for the lady to wait for me,
Today again it denied it.
Today again my heart made a wish,
Today again I explained it, But I failed, my heart won,
There is a lady awaiting me On the porch inviting me home.

58. Unaware

I don't know why I love you
But I loved with all my heart
There are many reasons for not loving,
But there are no reasons to love.
If you ask me how much my life is worth,
I will say it is as much as our love Because
without your love my life would not exist
Every letter reads your love
Every trait our love has shown in you
All the beauties of the world put you aside,
I want you because I loved you not with many eyes.
With my mind.

ABOUT POET

Prof. Kaluvakunta Ramakrishna has written about two hundred poems during the last two decades that have reflected the conflicts of Socio-cultured life of human beings. He is the reciepent of Indira Gandhi National Award for NSS service at SRR Govt. Arts & Science College(A), Karimnagar in 2013.

He was awarded Bharat Bhasha Bhushan National Literary Award from Akhila bharateeya Bhasha Sahitya Sammelan, Bhopal, Madhya Pradesh.

He is a poet, critic, writer and motivational speaker. He did his Masters in Telugu, English and Sanskrit languages. He obtained M.Phil from University of Hyderabad and Ph.D. from Osmania University. He was conferred D.Litt. **At present he is extending his services as Principal, S.R.R Govt. Arts & ScienceCollege(A), Karimnagar , Telangana state.** He rendered 25 years' service in the Collegiate Education. He received 4 Gold medals in MA (Telugu) from Osmania University, Hyderabad. He presented research papers in **45 National seminars** and published **58 research articles** in scholarly journals and edited anthologies.

He is on the editorial board forJunior and Senior Intermediate Telugu Textbooks. He edited Adarsha Darshanam (Vidwan Krishnamacharya's 60 years Literary book). Amrutha Murthi (Life

History of Sant Sukandara Swamy). Vignana Deepika, Sahithi Chetana, Shatavahana Poetry and Maneti Kavitha. He published Sri Vasara Saraswathi Shatakam. Akshara Deepalu, Prema Naa Chirunama, Kaluvukunta Naneelu and Haritha Yatra, Karona Naneelu, Fragment of life, He is Editorial Board Member for U.G. Telugu Text books, Higher Education in India etc.

His works of Telugu Literary Criticism include Sahithya Souhithyam, Aalokana, Vimarsha Vignanam and Sri Krishan Yathindra Jeeyar Rachanalu – Parisheelana.

Presently, he is the Syndicate member, Satavahana University, Karimnagar.

He guided for PH.D in Telugu Dravidian University,Kuppam,Andhrapradesh.

His Recent Publication : **HIGHER EDUCTAION IN INDIA, PROBLEMS AND PROSPECTUS WITH SPECIAL REFERENCE TO TELANGANA STATE. 2022**

Prof.K.Ramakrishna

ABOUT TRANSLATOR

Preethi Richards, a nature poet whose central theme of poetry revolves around nature.

She made her debut with **"NAKED LOVE"** and continued her journey through most celebrated book named **"SOLITARY SOUL - sings poetry"**.

Her Latest book is with title **MEMORIES - From my Land** which is featured in both Online & offline stores Globally and was an immediate hit.

She is a recipient of **INDIAN NOBLE AWARDS,**

UNITED INDIA NATIONAL AWARD, and TEALNGANA BOOK STATE HOLDER

She is making her Debut as Translator with **"ECHOES OF LOVE"** .

She resembles an old soul living in young body with her poems.

Her both books were listed in the famous book site BARNES AND NOBLE.

Her creative urges towards nature have won appreciation from many.